GOD'S MASTERPIECE

GOD'S MASTERPIECE

MARY OLUFUNMILAYO ADEKSON

New Harbor Press
RAPID CITY, SOUTH DAKOTA

Adekson/New Harbor Press
16601 Mt. Rushmore Rd, Ste 3288
Rapid City, SD 57701
www.NewHarborPress.com

Ordering Information:
Quantity sales. Special discounts are available on quantity purchases by corporations, associations, and others. For details, contact the "Special Sales Department" at the address above.

God's Masterpiece/Mary Olufunmilayo Adekson. —1st ed.
ISBN 978-1-63357-332-1

CONTENTS

*God's Masterpiece is dedicated to the Almighty God
who made all of us in His own image.*

New life in Christ-----miraculous
That we're not bound by sin !
The power of God-----how glorious
That we've been changed within
(Sper)

PREFACE

Our God is good, great and holy. This God loves us so dearly and He will do anything to make us remain in His image for as long as we are here. We need to adore God and ensure that we look to God to live a life perfect in Him. God said in His Words in Psalm 82 verse 6 that, "I said You are gods, and all of you are children of the most High." He also said in Psalm 138 verse 8a that He shall perfect all those things that concern us. But since we were born into Adam's sin, we fall short. But God sent His Son to redeem us and bring us to fit into His perfect image. The tendency is for us to want to go our own ways and do things in our sinful nature. God is calling us to come back and be aligned to His image as He redeemed us with Jesus Christ's blood from our sins. *God's Masterpiece* will give you an insight to think and come back to this sinless state and see yourself as His masterpiece with the help of Our Lord Jesus Christ and the Holy Spirit. So, be encouraged.

Acknowledgements

I thank God as always for the inspiration to write *God's Masterpiece.* Holy Spirit: Thank you always for your help and assistance with helping me in putting all the words together perfectly. You have been my guide throughout my life. I am always in awe about your leadings.

I am grateful to all those who encourage me over the years and stood by me so I can become God's Masterpiece here on this journey.

WHO IS MARY OLUFUNMILAYO ADEKSON ?

My childhood was full of spiritual adventures after I accepted the Lord Jesus Christ as my Lord and Savior when I was 8 years old. My life has not been the same ever since I encountered my Lord. I remember clinging tightly to the beautiful picture of the lilies (Matthew 6: 28-30) that my Sunday School Teacher gave us after her sermon to us about God's provision and care, that unforgettable and divine Sunday. I determined and resolved in my heart to love this Almighty Father who takes care of the lilies in the field which are here today and destroyed tomorrow. I possessed a childlike belief that this God is going to take care of me throughout my life here on earth. The rest is history. I was transformed with a dramatic vision of God with a personal relationship with Him and God has proved Himself to me over all these years and He still continues to deliver on His Promises. I go to Him for answers for all situations in my life. He listens and answers my cries, petitions and prayers. I am also grateful to my Godly earthly father, late Papa Gabriel Omodele Ekundiya Asanbe-Williams who stood by me during trials, troubles and tribulations. As Psalm 112 verse 6b says, "The righteous shall be in everlasting remembrance." You are remembered for all your fatherly care for me and my family.

I am a walking miracle because of Jesus Christ who loves me. I am grateful to You God for the opportunity to know You and be a living witness for You. I stand ! I stand in awe of You !! Holy God to whom all praise is due !!! I stand in awe of You !!!! Thank you so much God. You are AWESOME and GREAT !!!!!

INTRODUCTION

If we all know from a tender age that we are all God's Masterpiece, it will make a big difference in the way we live our lives and relate to others around us. This knowledge will allow us to speak when we should and also to hold our peace when we should. We will not be timid. We will be as bold as a lion and we will be able to put everything into their proper perspectives. Our thinking will be different. If we know that we are winners, warriors, precious child of God who has been forgiven, we will live our lives holding our heads high. God loves us. He made us in His image and wants us to behave like mini gods (Psalm 82:6) that we are. He sent His Son to redeem us after Adam and Eve fell to sin. So, we are the redeemed of the Lord. Let the redeemed of the Lord say so. We are redeemed. We are redeemed. Praise the Lord. *God's Masterpiece* will help those who are downcast and esteem themselves as "less than." It will encourage and help those who are struggling with their self-image. *God's Masterpiece* will assist you to know that your Papa in Heaven really loves you and want you to be a success. So, cherish it. Read it over and over again. God's Masterpiece is written to make you know that you are fearfully and wonderfully made (Psalm 139:14) in God's image and that you are one of a kind in the world. You are the only person like you. Not knowing you are God's masterpiece can make you end up in the wrong relationships, jobs or in other avenues in life where God has not destined you to be. *God's Masterpiece* will also depict God's power and greatness as He propels you to overcome the deliberate or non-deliberate plans and intentions of your enemies. Don't allow those who feel inadequate in themselves to project their inadequate feelings to you by putting you down. Hold your head high as a son or daughter who is made in the image of God your Father. Remember that whatever your size: small, medium, large or extra-large, you are perfect in your Father's sight.

[1]

Who are you?

God made you in His image (Genesis 1:26). You are unique! You are a unique expression of God's lovely design. No other person is like you! Psalms 139 verse 14 says "I will praise You for I am fearfully and wonderfully made; Marvelous are Your works. And that my soul knows very well." Psalm 71 verse 7 says: "I have become as a wonder unto many, but you are my strong refuge," and verse 6 says "By you I have been upheld from birth. You are He who took me out of my mother's womb." In first Peter 2 verse 9, we are referred to as a chosen generation, special people. You are called the chosen and the beloved. Paul said in Ephesians 2 verse 10 that, "for we are His workmanship created in Christ Jesus for good works, which God prepared beforehand that we should work in them." Another translation of this verse says you are "God's masterpiece." You are referred to as the replica of Jesus Christ (Romans 8:29). As you can see from all the above Word of God, God loves you just the way you are because He made you as a unique being: One of a kind. Can you believe one thing: You are the only one like you in the universe. Halleluia! Doesn't that blow your mind. There is no one that has your fingerprints, your talents, your individuality, your intelligence, your voice, your looks and even more unique characteristics. So, my dear brothers and sisters: Don't miss the path God has mapped out for you personally. Your purpose gifting journey and time-frame is ordained by God before you came here. Lysa Terkeurst reiterated that, "God created you on purpose with a purpose (in mind)" (Encouragement for Today). So, don't squander your talents. Listen to the leading of the Holy Spirit. Use all that God has made you for, so that God can happily say to you when you see Him face to face: Welcome good and faithful servant. Don't you ever allow anyone to define who you are. Don't let anyone make you into a victim because to your Father, you are one of a kind: a unique darling. Stop comparing yourself to others in terms of what you can do or what you cannot do. Galatians 3 verse 26 says: "For you are all sons (and also daughters) of God through faith in Christ Jesus." God does not want us to forget who we are: His children, His precious children. So, don't suffer from identity amnesia. Focus on the positive things about yourself. Skip all the negatives as God your maker does every day. Don't give up your right as the unique beloved of God Almighty. You are brother and sister of Jesus Christ who redeemed you with His precious Blood. Hebrews 10 verse 14 says that you are made perfect in the Lord. God has established you in Jesus Christ (2 Corinthians 1:21). You were sealed with the Holy Spirit of promise (Ephesians 1:13). Don't let your present circumstances or disappointments sway you or make you to lose your confidence in your Father who make you a unique being. Let your faith be strengthened in the fact that you are one of a kind.

[2]

WHO DOES GOD SAY YOU ARE ?

Our Lord said you are children of the Almighty God (Galatians 3:26). He says that you are forgiven (Acts 10:43). You are reconciled to God (2 Corinthians 5:18-19). You are joint heirs with Jesus Christ (Romans 8:16-17; Galatians 3:26). And that you are God's adopted children (Galatians 4:4-7). You are God's witnesses and ambassadors (Matthew 28:19-20; 2 Corinthians 5:20); and that you are destined to be like His Son (Romans 8:29). You are more than a conqueror (Romans 8:37). You are blessed because you trust in the Lord (Jeremiah 17:7-8; Psalm 1:1-3). You are loved: For God so loved you that He gave His only begotten Son for you, that since you believed in Him you will not perish but have everlasting eternal life (John 3:16). You are warriors like Gideon and Daniel (Judges 6:12b; Daniel 4:25d). You are women and men of valor like Esther, Deborah, Job, Joseph, Peter, Gideon, Shadrach, Meshach and Abednego. You are men and women of faith like Abraham, Lydia, Ruth, Enoch, Noah, Elijah and Elisha to mention just a few of the saints of God who are warriors and faithful God believers. You are a person after God's heart like David. You are a fighter like Jacob. You are a prayer warrior like Daniel, Paul and our greatest example Jesus Christ Our Lord and Savior. These should keep you secure in the Lord who brought you here. The Lord God

Almighty says you are also a winner. Psalm 18 verses 18 to 19 says "they confronted me in the day of my calamity; But the Lord was my support He also brought me out into a broad place He delivered me because He delighted in me." And verses 29 to 30 of the same Psalm says: "For by You I can run against a troop, by my God I can leap over a wall... He is a shield to all who trust in Him. The Psalmist is saying that all those who put their confidence in God's help and support will leap over a wall. They will run and not be weary, they will walk and not faint (Isaiah 40:31). David had a winner's attitude when he confronted Goliath and said, "the Lord who delivered me from the paw of the lion and from the paw of the bear will deliver me from the hand of the Philistine" (I Samuel 17:37). Daniel told the king: " My God sent His angel and shut the lions' mouths, so they have not hurt me....... "(Daniel 7:21). Shadrach, Meshach and Abednego portrayed their winner's badge by saying: "If that is the case our God whom we serve is able to deliver us from the burning furnace and He will deliver us from your hand, O king" (Daniel 3:17). Elijah was another example of a winner as he called down fire on Mount Carmel (I Kings 18). Joseph's winning attitude graced him into Egypt's prime minister position despite his trials and travails. As you read the Word of God identify winners and associate yourself with them and cultivate a winning attitude towards all obstacles or challenges that come your way. Reexamine your life and face your life as the child of the Almighty who has made you a winner. With God on your side you will scale mountains of daily problems, adversity, sufferings, and struggles and subsequently become a winner. Tell yourself daily that you are a winner and warrior and all these other attributes that God bestow on you and start living as a winner and as God's specially endowed child because God sees you as a winner. You can do this by immersing yourself in the Word of God and claiming His promises for you and your household. Pray, praise, and share His Word with others who need to know Him. Let your words and actions project you as a winner everyday of your life. Stop whining. Stop grumbling. Stop complaining. Start winning. Overcome hurt, shame, guilt, doubt, covetousness, world-liness, love of money, pride, regret, and other negative attitudes and replace them with a winning warrior and successful child of God attitude. And you know what, believe me, God says that you are blessed and highly favored and also that you will do great exploits (Daniel 11:32).

[3]

HOW DO YOU THINK OF YOURSELF AS GOD'S CHILD? WHY ARE YOU HERE ?

Some people think that God judges them and look sternly on them as an earthly Father does. Far from it. God sees you as His perfect image. This is how you should see yourself as I pointed out in the previous chapter. Do not sell yourself short. Think of yourself as an overcomer. Do not see yourself as a looser. The way you see yourself will portray how you relate to God as Father. You are God's special son and daughter. So, start seeing and thinking of yourself that way from today. Walk with your head high. Think of yourself as a person who can achieve great and mighty things. You are here on this earth to succeed and be a blessing to others. So, think and act this way. Your success in life depends on your attitude to life and to all the situations you encounter. To survive and succeed in life, you must take control of your attitudes to all the situations that come your way. How can you do this? You must have the attitude and mindset of Jesus Christ. This means you must set your minds on things above (Colossians 3:2), not on worldly things. Some people like money and material things. That is not the mindset of Jesus Our Savior. You must flee from lusts and from holding on tightly to material things and things of the world. You must have the same attitude that Jesus had (Philippians 2:5). What was Christ's attitude? He looked to His Father for answers in everything. He followed God's will. And that shaped His responses to different things and the world. How did He do this while He was on earth? By staying in contact with His Father through prayers for direction. You will notice that Jesus always set out to pray while other people were sleeping. You can be in tune with your Father by calling on Him in prayer and by yielding to the Holy Spirit when He leads you. The Holy Spirit will guide you to do all things if you believe and have accepted Jesus as your Savior. To yield to Him, you must have a Christ-like attitude. Jesus promised and gave us the Holy Spirit: the Comforter and Director of our lives. All we have to do as believers is heed the Holy Spirit and our attitude will be like that of Our Lord Jesus Christ.

There are few things in life we have control over. But we can control our attitude especially since we, as born-again Christians, have the inspiration of the Holy Spirit. Dispel fear. Welcome changes and dare to believe and have a Christ-like positive attitude to all situations that you encounter. Dare to be a Daniel in the lions' den, a Joseph in prison, an Elijah, an Elisha, a David as he encountered Goliath, a Paul as he went through so many challenges, a Peter the Rock, and of course Our Lord Jesus Christ who suffered and rose again to save you and me, in your daily attitude to life. Dare to have an attitude like that of Shadrach, Meshach and Abednego who informed the king that they were not going to bow down to his god even if it means death. So, my dear, start maintaining a Christ-like attitude today. Remember, you are more than conquerors through Jesus Christ who gives you strength and who will help you develop a positive, Christ-like attitude. Ask Him and He will assist you starting from now. When you ask He gives you your hearts' desires. May God help you as you pray for the right Christ-like attitude that will last you throughout your time here on earth. Amen. Remember, that you are gifted to be a gift to the world.

[4]

KNOW YOUR IDENTITY SO YOU DO NOT HAVE AN IDENTITY CRISIS.

Identity crisis occurs when individuals are teenagers, it can also occur during middle age and in later years of one's life. Questions occur and we as God's children should anchor our identity in Jesus Christ so we do not have an identity crisis. Our identity should become hidden in Jesus Christ. Anne Cetas of Our Daily Bread Ministries reiterated that, when "we deny our will and choose His instead. He transforms our thinking, our values, and our priorities to reflect what is acceptable to God—a vibrant relationship with Jesus." Romans 12 verse 2 says that you should not be conformed to this world but be transformed by the renewing of your mind that you may prove what is good and acceptable will of God. The peace of God will be yours when you put your trust in Jesus Christ (John 14:27). And "as you go through life, concentrate on the roses instead of the thorns" (Dave Branon, Our daily Bread Ministries). Oswald Chambers pointed out that you fulfill your spiritual destiny as soon as you obey Jesus Christ. That is, when you have a relationship with Him wholeheartedly. "If I obey Jesus Christ, the redemption of God will flow through me to the lives of others, because behind the deed of obedience is the reality of Almighty God" (Oswald Chambers). Because in God we live and move and have our being (Acts 17:28). One thing I want you to remember is that your identity is securely linked to Jesus Christ once you accept Him as Lord and Savior. So, don't let the devil steal your identity because Jesus Christ has come to give us life and that life abundantly while the devil comes to steal and destroy (John 10:10). The enemy of this world seeks after your identity daily. The devil wants to drag you to hell with him and its cohorts after confusing you when he steals your identity. Preserve your identity every second of the day. Hide your identity in Our Lord Jesus Christ by being vigilant and watchful because the devil and its cohorts are roaming around regularly and seeking whom they will devour (I Peter 5:8). They are our arch enemies and identity stealers. Be careful as Jesus warns us because there are people, things and temptations that will constantly attempt to lure and entice you away from the real you, your true identity in Christ. Your true identity must be securely shaped in concrete, solidified foundation of Jesus Christ because you are a chosen generation (1 Peter 2:9). And Jesus Christ is Our Rock, Our Solid and Immovable Foundation whom we can come close to through His Word, embracing its truth and daily calling on God for help and praising Him. Almighty God the creator of the universe and your Father, the Sustainer, the Ruler of the World, says that you are His child and that your identity is intact because you are fearfully and wonderfully made in His image (Psalms 139:14) and securely anchored in Him through Our Lord Jesus Christ. Our Lord says that you are very special, you are one of a kind, a unique being known before the foundation of the world (Psalm 139:13-16; Psalm 71:3-7). Once we know Him and are empowered by Him, we can trust Him to fight our battles on our behalf as we live for Him (Psalm 24:8). God fights for us and sustains our identity through the battles, struggles, adversities and sufferings that we go through in the world. We become strengthened through all these tribulations. Therefore, focus on God, your Creator who will continue to keep your identity hidden in Himself and intact in the midst of life's battles and wars and keep you securely until you see His face (Proverbs 4:25-27). As a teenager you are growing to become a masterpiece that God created you to be. So, during times of doubts and waverings, stand with Jesus. Do not listen to negative talks or negative proddings from friends. Make friends with those who know and love Jesus Christ. Immerse yourself in the Word of God and pray for God's guidance in every move you make. Remember, you are growing physically, psychologically and emotionally. Your bodies are being formed by God who created you. So, talk to Him about your worries and insecurities not to anyone else because He knitted you together in your Mama's womb. He will help you get through the turmoils and problems of teenage years. Exercise, eat right, nourish yourself in the Word of God and surround yourself with Godly people. As Solomon says in Ecclesiastes 3, there is time for everything, this too shall pass, and you will get through the normal crisis of teenage years. Drown yourself in positive Godly things. Do not dabble into anything ungodly or negative that you will regret later in life. This is your time to be an ambassador for Jesus Christ in your school and with friends. Also, as a middle aged Christian, there will be times of struggle and doubts about your current achievements and aspirations. Do not let discouragement take you from your focus on your Creator and why you are here. Celebrate what you have been able to do so far and make plans for further achievements you intend to pursue with God's help. Cherish your relationships. That is, relationships with God, your mate if you are married, your family members and your church community. Read and ruminate on the Word, Pray and Praise God for His past blessings and look forward to more future blessings. God is excellent. He will never leave you nor forsake you (Deuteronomy 31:6). And for those that are retired, thank God for all you have done in your life so far. Count your blessings. Name them one by one and it will surprise all what the Lord has done for you. Do not let the devil pin you down with what you have not done in your life. Volunteer with young ones and share your knowledge of God and experience with them. Do not allow the devil or any negative person to steer you away from your God-given identity which has been solidified in Jesus Christ. Read the Word, Pray and Praise God. Remember, God is the only true one that gives you an authentic identity. The devil gives false identity because he is fake like his followers. So, don't take the bait. Remain loyal to the Original. Don't give in to the powers of darkness that are always working deviously to get you to detour from standing firm on Christ Our Rock and Foundation. Stand (Ephesians 6:14), and, put on the whole armor of God (Ephesians 6:10-18). Be steadfast and immovable holding securely to your identity in Jesus Christ. May God's hand be in your life. May you always be watchful and know that since your identity is in Christ nothing can move you or snatch you away from Him. When you have doubts about who you are defer to God and read the Holy Bible. Pray and praise and look at God's Words that assure you that you are embedded in Him. When confusion comes pray and remember the son or daughter of whom you are: The Almighty God. He knows you intimately and also loves you dearly. Jesus Christ is also praying for you. Stand strong. Do not give in to negative people. Relate with Christ-centered positive friends and family members for encouragement. The Lord who knows you intimately and created you to succeed will be beside you as you work through the turmoils of identity crisis. You should remind yourself that the potter knows the clay and the pots He made are beautiful and intact. Since you are His Handiwork you are beautiful and intact. Do not let confusion arise about your identity. Let your anchor be secure on Jesus Christ.

[5]

DO NOT ALLOW THE DEVIL AND THE WORLD TO DERAIL YOU FROM WHAT GOD HAS ENDOWED YOU WITH

Do you know that as an anointed and blood-bought child of God, that God's love is eternal, infallible and unfazed in such a way that His plans for your life cannot be derailed or denied, once you accept Jesus as your Lord and Savior and hold true to your standing in the Lord. Yes, hold true to your standing in Him, God dominates the story of your life. We are tempted to believe that our troubles direct the story like when Goliath boasted in front of the Israelites and loom large to stir up fear and confusion (I Samuel 17). That is how the devil and its cohorts and all the powers of darkness boast and loom large in the midst of our troubles, travails, sufferings and tribulations. But we should be like David in front of all these Goliaths. Because when David showed up proclaiming the sovereignty and supremeness of God, Goliath became a dead dog. So, will all your travails and enemies become dead dogs when you trust in Your Maker and Deliverer. And NONE of the plans God has for you can be derailed, denied or changed if you allow God to reign supreme in your life. But you have to learn to speak it out like David did, and proclaim that your God is larger than your problems, sufferings and temptations (I Samuel 17: 45 & 41-50). What concerns or problems threaten to overwhelm you these days? Speak the Word of God into them. And where do these Words come from? How do you acquire these Words? By spending time in the Word of God daily. Memorize some key verses that can be used as dynamites to destroy temptations, words, negative thoughts that the devil and its cohorts bring to your minds as Goliaths. Remember, Satan was not there when God ordained and wrote and laid down the story of your life. As a liar that he is, he will even pretend to shower you with some words from the Holy Bible to lure you to believe he is authentic. The Spirit of God will hold the truth and counteract all counterfeits and proclaim that if you surrender totally to God, Satan cannot change the story of your life. So, do not buy into Satan's false words because he and its cohorts come to steal, kill and destroy. But remember, Jesus came to give us life and in abundance (John 10:10). So, my dear, be on the Lord's side totally not partially; not one leg in and another leg out, and He will give you abundant life because His promises are Yea and Amen. So, stick with the Lord. The maker knows everything about what He made. God never disappoints. He made you fearfully and wonderfully (Psalm 139:14). His miracles will manifest in your life if you allow Him to reign supreme in all your undertakings of your life. Make Him Master of your life. Make Him pilot of the plane of your life and His plans to make you a success will not be thwarted (Jeremiah 29:11-13). And I say as His beloved like you: "None of His plans for our lives can be derailed, stopped or denied."

The psalmist says you are fearfully and wonderfully made in Your Father's image. So therefore, you will always be a success, no matter what the devil says or plans. I am always happy to read Paul's advice and admonitions. Like all of us and even more so than us, Paul had the scars to show for his failures and successes and because of these we can slow down and listen to his advice and admonitions. My dear, there are many success-robbers that are continuously fighting for your attention to get you discouraged and make you fear what the future holds for you. Guilt, regret, fear, self-pity and shame can keep you from attaining your crown. You need to let past mistakes rest and die in the bosom of yesteryears. Be assured that God's will in your life will manifest if you let go of your past. Stop clinging to the past mistakes of your life like Paul said in Philippians 3 verses 12 to 15, where he said that It's not like he has attained the best, but he is still pressing forward to attain the prize, the crown. So, step forward, don't look back, move forward, fight on. Don't look back. Don't be like Lot's wife. Keep your focus on the future: Focus and attain the bright tomorrow that God has stored securely for you and your family. Rely on the Holy Spirit for peace, strength, and patience because patience builds character (James 1:3-4). Work through your emotions and avoid basking in glow of regrets, frustrations, self-pity, fear, that can lead to paralysis and thereby prevent you from moving forward to reach your Christ ordained goals. Success-robbers can prevent you from getting your crown when you see Our Savior face to face. Concentrate on God: The Author and Finisher of your faith. When you falter or fall, stand up again. Do not let success-robbers keep you from praying, reading the Word, praising God or fellowshiping with other believers. Praise anyway. Do not let success-robbers keep you down. Do not let discouragement steal your joy. Move forward and serve your Lord. Listen to the voice of the Holy Spirit. Follow the will of God for your life. Remember: It's your Father's will to give you the best in this life and in the life to come. So, run away from success-robbers and cling to success-lovers: Prayer, meditating on the Word of God and Praising Your Creator (Proverbs 24:16). The Word in Hebrews 6 verses 9 to 10; 2 Corinthians 5 verse 21; Isaiah 54 verse 17; Romans 8 verses 31 to 39 and Philippians 4 verse 13 will help steer you away from the world and its enticements. Remember: Your Father loves you and He has made you a success. The devil, the world, success-robbers cannot snatch you from God or steal your identity. Beware of individuals who will make you feel or think of you as "less than" who your Creator made you to be.

[6]

BE SECURE AND MATURE IN THE LORD.

Time spent with God, family and friends are valuable. Dr. J. L. Parker sums up what makes a mature Christian as: ability to deal constructively with reality, that is as he said, mature people don't kid themselves; they have the ability to adapt quickly to change; and they possess freedom from the symptoms of tension and anxiety (in other words, they cast all their burdens on the Lord); they are more satisfied with giving than receiving; they also have the ability to relate to others with consistency; and they have the ability to use the adrenaline created by anger in a positive way, rather than lose their temper and add to the problem (they are angry but sin not, and they do not let the sun go down with their anger). If you do all the above, you will have a mature mindset that will keep you secure in the Lord. As a prayer warrior myself, I find out that prayer and reading the word of God help me keep things in proper perspective and become steadfast and mature in the Lord. Jesus' Words in John 15 verse 5 that Jesus is the vine and we are the branches aids us in holding firmly to the vine so we can bear fruits. So, be anchored into the vine and your branch will be juicy. Acts 17 verse 28 reiterates that in Him we live and move and have our being. Colossians 1 verse 17 says we are inherent in God. Paul enumerates in first Corinthians 2 verse 6 that they speak Godly wisdom among mature men and women. He added in first Corinthians 14 verse 20 that, we as God's children should be mature in understanding the Words of God and His laws, not behaving like immature children. And in Philippians 3 verse 15 Paul admonished us further to have a mature mind. The Word of God will help you as you navigate the world and they will keep you secure in the Lord with the right mature mind. Moreover, the Holy Spirit will aid you to become more mature in God daily. God keeps you secure in His arms, hold you in the palms of His Hands and underneath you are His everlasting arms (Deuteronomy 33:27). When you heed God's Word, walk maturely in His statutes, you will dwell securely under His strong arms. When you become mature in the Lord, the dominating power of the world, the flesh, and the devil are all brought to their knees in front of the power and strength of God's redemptive influence. Your maturity and security stem from God's strength and power. Wisdom from above help solidify and establish your maturity and security in the Lord of the Universe. It helps you live a life of victory as God's Masterpiece. "The wisdom from above is first pure, then peaceable, gentle, willing to yield, full of mercy and good fruits, without partiality and without hypocrisy"(James 3:17).

[7]

YOU ARE THE APPLE OF GOD'S EYE

God says that whoever touches you and me, touches the apple of His eye (Psalm 17:8; Proverbs 7:2; Deuteronomy 32:10; Zechariah 2:8). This solid fact should keep you singing and dancing daily for the rest of your life. Nobody can touch you because you are God's anointed and His prophet (Psalm 105:15; Psalm 139). You are Kings, Queens and Priests. You are so special to your Almighty Father. So, ask yourself: What makes me so special? Of course, the answer is obvious. The fact that you have accepted Jesus Christ as Your Lord and Savior gives you access to God as your Father since God loves His Son and sent Him to die for your sins. He counts us worthy and righteous because of this. God's love for us is pure, perfect, and rooted in the way He loves His Son. John 3 verse 16 says, "For God so loved the world that He gave His only begotten Son that whoever believes in Him should not perish but have everlasting life." And John 6 verse 33 says Jesus is the bread of life that came down from heaven to give life to the world. So, wherever you go in this world God's eyes go with you and follow you to protect and care for you because His promise is: He will neither leave you nor forsake you (Deuteronomy 31:6). He has excellent plans for your life whatsoever you are engaged in right now in your abode here. All you have to do is seek Him and His righteousness and all other things will be added to you (Matthew 6:33). And Our Father will rejoice over you (Zephaniah 3:17) and keep you as the apple of His eye and hide you under the shadow of His wings (Psalm 17:8). Oswald Chambers summed up God's love and presence with us this way: "God walked with man and talked with him, He told him (and her) His mind (through the Holy Spirit) and showed (her or) him the precise path which he must walk in order to enjoy the happiness He had ordained for him (or her). He rejoiced in the fulness of His nature over man (and woman) as His child, the offspring of His love. He left nothing unrevealed to man (or woman), He loved him (or her)." So, what are you waiting for to be counted worthy of this never-ending love if you don't think you are counted worthy now? To be counted as apple of God's eye bow your head now or kneel where you are and ask Jesus to be your Lord and Savior. And you will be secure in God's Arms and become the apple of God's eye and all things will become new in your life (2 Corinthians 5:17). If you are already His Child and have accepted Jesus Christ as your Lord and Savior, continue in His Love by being pure and being led by the Holy Spirit. Immerse yourself in the Word of God and pray as you continue your walk with the Lord within God's congregation. As apple of God's eye you will have a victorious and productive life.

[8]

DO WHAT PLEASES GOD AND RUN AWAY FROM WHAT THE WORLD WANTS YOU TO BE.

Don't let the world determine or shape who you are. God has the final say about you because you are His Masterpiece. He is the potter. You are the clay (Isaiah 29:16; 64:8; Jeremiah 18:1-9; Romans 9:14-24). He molds you into His perfect son and daughter. The world has put down certain guidelines for its inhabitants that make some people falter if they do not look at God's guidelines. One of them is regarding relationships. Some have sought fulfillments in the wrong relationships to the detriment of seeking the Lord. Yes, you need other people in your lives. But you need God first. You also need to let your relationships bring honor to the Almighty God throughout your life here on earth. Anything less than that will bring you misery. Your relationship with God should be your number one priority. There are some guidelines set by the world about being single. Being single can lead to wholeness and establishing a uniqueness in God that will eventually help you in your marriage if you so desire it later. You establish yourself in singleness and eventually develop a positive self-esteem during the process. Enjoying personal intimate relationship with yourself first will help you develop into a whole person. That is loving yourself, how God made you and who God made you to be. Whether single or married, serve the Lord and others and be pleased with yourself. Be pure, holy and steadfast in the Lord. Do not follow the tenets of the world. Oswald Chambers reiterated that, "it is better to enter into life maimed but lovely in God's sight than to appear lovely to man's eyes but lame to God's." Jesus Christ also said if your right hand causes you to sin cut it off because it is better to go into eternal life with one hand than to go to hell with two hands (Matthew 5:30). Remember, being single is neither a sin nor a taboo. Paul was single. He wrote the epistles that help us grow today as Christians. Your usefulness does not depend on being married or being single. It depends on your availability to be God's child and serve His children. So, do not let the world deceive you that being married or going in the way of the world are the only ways to self-fulfillment. So, set your affections on things above not on earthly things (Colossians 3:2). And if you are called to be married, spend time with God and your family in chastity. But remember do not be unequally yoked with unbelievers (2 Corinthians 6:13-18). Your relationships should reflect what the Word of God depicts and teaches us.

[9]

MAXIMIZE YOUR GOD-GIVEN POTENTIAL AND GET YOUR BREAKTHROUGHS

Learn to commit your ways to the Lord from a young age and your plans will succeed (Proverbs 16:3). Each of us should use whatever gift we have received from God maximally to glorify His Holy Name (1 Peter 4:10; Ephesians 4:11-13; 1 Corinthians 12: 8-10, 28-30; Romans 12:6-8). Paul highlighted different offices that are designated for us as God's children in Ephesians 4 verse 11; and Romans 12 verses 6 to 8, he lists the spiritual gifts we are endowed with. 1 Peter 4 verses 10 to 11 classified the gifts into those of speaking and serving. Paul instructed us that if teaching is our gift we should use it to build up, stabilize, unite, equip and mature the church and God's people (Ephesians 4: 11-13). Each of us should pray and ask God to show us what our God-given gift is and how we can use this gift to glorify His Name in the world. Young or old we have all been endowed with different gifts. Once you identify your gift, pray like Isaiah did that God will make you pure and holy to use your God-given gift. Use your gift to glorify His Name not for selfish ambition or self-glorification.

When God gives you a gift, He backs you up with all the resources you will need to use that gift. Joseph, Daniel, David, Elijah, Paul, Moses and all our Godly fore-fathers used their gifts to glorify God and they were blessed for doing so. Surrender to God and use your gifts and talents every day to make His Name great. To recognize and utilize your gifts, you must immerse yourself in His Word, pray incessantly and listen to the Holy Spirit as He leads you. Ask God to show you His blueprint for your life and pray for success in all your life's endeavors. Let God have His way in your life as you use your gifts to honor Him. Let the joy of the Lord be your strength (Nehemiah 8:10). God will empower you to be what He called you to be when you make Him the Master of your life. Like Jeremiah, He knew you before you were formed in the womb (Jeremiah 1:5-9) and you were fearfully and wonderfully crafted in your Mama's womb (Psalm 139:14). Be humble and do not compare your gifts or talents with those of others because God knows your capability before He gave you your gift and talents that only you can use to glorify His Name. God called you apart since there is no other person like you in the universe. So, tap into His power and use your gift to make your Almighty Father proud. You are gifted to gift your fellow human beings. Generously give your time, talent, gifts and efforts to advance God's Kingdom and you will be on your way to embrace your God-given destiny. Good Luck as you identify and use your gift and talent. The basic points for us is to Repent and Believe God, act on what God says and you will get your breakthrough. That means study and meditate on the Word of God and pray. You will be like Joseph --- the prison could not keep him from the palace. You will be like Abraham and Sarah for whom God broke through impossible physical barriers to give them Isaac a son of promise. You will be like the Israelites at the mouth of the Red Sea where God supernaturally drowned the Egyptians army who were after them. You will be like Gideon who defeated the Midianites with a handful of men. You will be like Paul and Silas ---- who prayed and praised God and the Holy Ghost came down. You will be like Daniel who supernaturally came out of the lions' den alive. You will be like Shadrach, Meshach and Abednego who came out of the king's fiery furnace unscathed. You will be like Mordecai who came out of the king's noose unhanged. And you will be like Our Lord Jesus Christ who supernaturally came out of the tomb alive. And more Holy Bible stories that you have read about God's supernatural breakthroughs. Just say it. Learn to use the Word of God and breakthrough will all be yours. Remember: As I always tell everyone: God is excellent all the time and He will supernaturally give you your breakthroughs. No matter what the devil and its cohorts plan and scheme, God is going to see you through all your difficulties and sufferings. Because you believe in Jesus Christ as your Lord and Savior, and you are God's masterpiece, you are overcomers. So, rest in the Lord, don't fret because your miracles are here. God's Hand is in your life and your family's and He will supernaturally give you an abundance and lots of breakthroughs. Amen. Have faith in God's preeminence.

[10]

FULFILL YOUR PURPOSE IN LIFE WITH GOD'S HELP, JESUS CHRIST'S CHEERING HOPE AND THE HOLY SPIRIT'S ASSISTANCE.

What kind of person are you growing into? Humble, patient, kind, tolerant, grateful, forgiving, peaceful, loving (Galatians 5:22-26). How are you growing? Are you growing to resemble Our Savior? Do you have a resemblance and likeness reflected in a kind old face --- that is, do you have a likeness and resemblance of Our Lord and Savior? Are you growing lovelier every day? (Philippians 4:8). Despite wrinkles, blemishes, and other disfigurements, do you have marks of inner transformation? May God help us to grow daily to be like Jesus Christ. This can only be possible when we allow Our Savior to transform our hearts. Let Him do a heart surgery in you. This is only possible when you open your heart to Him like a little child because there is nothing like the beauty of a loving and humble heart. Paul tells us in Romans 13 verse 14 to "clothe {ourselves} with the Lord Jesus Christ. Romans 8 verse 29 tells us to become a picture of Jesus

Christ, a replica (1 John 3:2). "Be truly righteous and holy (Ephesians 4:24). Grow in the Lord and wait for complete transformation at His coming (1 Corinthians 15:49-53). One thing you should understand is that it is a process (2 Cor 3:18) that you can allow to happen and open up to now so that when you finally see His face you will be exactly like Him. How can this be possible? Spend time in the Word, Pray to God using Jesus Christ's Name, spend time with other genuine believers, tell others about your love of God the Father, God the Son and God the Holy Spirit. If there is any sin in your life, repent and pray that God transform you to be holy as Our Savior is holy. Believe me He understands, because He has been through this world where we are now. Make Jesus your personal friend. There is no friend like Him. What a friend we have in Jesus. Listen intimately and obediently to the Holy Spirit. The second question is what is your purpose in life? The steps of a good man are ordered by the Lord (Psalm 37:23). Write down your plan and fuel it up with specific actions. Ask yourself this question. Why am I here? How am I going to glorify God while I am here? Your plans will help you utilize your talents and make your dreams have realistic meanings. Follow your plans by setting up goals. Involve God and Jesus Christ and listen to the Holy Spirit's guidance as you follow through on your purpose and plans. Joseph highlighted what he was going to do during the famine in front of Pharaoh. Pharaoh was impressed that he noticed that God was with Joseph (Genesis 41:36-41). Your success comes when you have a purpose and plan to back up your dreams and the talent God has endowed you with. But seek God's face as you plan, and your purpose will be fulfilled because God make plans and purpose come to fruition. He will make you a success. Your plan should be seeking the Lord first and He will make you a success like David (a man after God's own heart)(Acts 13:22); like Daniel (a successful ardent prayer warrior); and like the three Hebrew sons (who got out of the king's fire without being scathed). Joshua identified his calling earlier in life and did not relent as Moses' servant. The Word of God says that, "but his servant Joshua the son of Nun, a young man, did not depart from the tabernacle" (Exodus 33:11c). Joshua eventually took the baton from Moses as the leader of Israel when Moses died. Identify your calling, have a plan with a timeline and have a purpose with God's help and with the Holy Spirit's nudging, and you will be sure to stand before great men (Proverbs 18:16). Our Lord our God is our strength, our hope, our love, our joy, our faith, our peace, our confidence, our courage and our friend. Our confidence comes from our relationship with Him. He is with us. We are His people. So, my dear, what is your purpose and plan in life? Align them with God and you are on your way to becoming God's Masterpiece on earth.

CONCLUSION

As a blood-bought child of the Almighty, I thank God for you, God's Masterpiece. As a masterpiece you are special and as I said earlier, you are one of a kind. No other person is like you on earth. So, from today, start walking with your head high everywhere you go. I know that as you were reading through this book you are thinking to yourself, Mary does not know the battle I am fighting. Yes, I know. Negative thoughts, success-robbers' comments, family members who do not know the Lord who bombard you with negative words and actions. The lists are extensive. When discouragement from feeling "less than" and feeling insecure or inadequate knocks on your door allow the God of courage who makes you a Masterpiece to answer the door. But I know one secret, if you can see yourself as God's Masterpiece and start thinking this way every second of the day, you will overcome and put all the naysayers to rest. You can only do this by immersing yourself in the Word of God, by praying incessantly and also praising God for all the blessings He bestowed into your life. Yes, little and big blessings. Read the Word of God about those who have succeeded in their walk with God. Read, study and memorize God's Word and work hard to apply them to your daily life. Have a deep time of prayer communicating intensely by pouring out what is in your heart to your Creator who has made you His Masterpiece (Matthew 11:29). Attend a Bible-based congregation. Run away from those negatively-inclined people where-ever they are and whoever they are. Surround yourself with those who are ardent believers in God. Yes, believe me, you are on your way to being the prized God's Masterpiece that you are. Finally, I leave you with Paul's words in Philippians 4 verse 8 that says "whatever things are true, whatever things are noble, whatever things are just, whatever things are pure, whatever things are lovely, whatever things are of good report, if there is any virtue and if there is anything praiseworthy—meditate on these things." And God: our refuge and strength and an ever-present help in trouble (Psalm 46:1) will see you through. Good Luck! It is working for me. It will work for you.

www.ingramcontent.com/pod-product-compliance
Lightning Source LLC
Chambersburg PA
CBHW031530040426
42445CB00009B/461